A Good Night for FREEDOM

BY

Barbara Olenyik Morrow

ILLUSTRATED BY

Leonard Jenkins

Levi Coffin
*"President
of the Underground
Railroad"*

Holiday House / New York

For Julia and Jim
—B. O. M.

For José Ortiz, my assistant
—L. J.

AUTHOR'S NOTE

The home of Levi and Catharine (Aunt Katy) Coffin in Fountain City (formerly Newport), Indiana, was a safe haven for about two thousand slaves escaping to freedom in Canada before the Civil War. Levi Coffin (1798–1877) was considered by many to be president of the Underground Railroad. Levi and Catharine were Quakers, members of a religious group opposed to slavery. The Coffin home was known as "Grand Central Station."

Writing years later about his work, Coffin described helping two slave girls from Tennessee. They arrived at his home one night, and by the next day, slave catchers were combing the area. Coffin was at his dry goods store when he learned the men were near. He ran home and told Aunt Katy, who hid the girls.

Through research I learned the names of the two runaways. In the spring of 1839, their master filed a lawsuit in an Indiana court, claiming he was cheated out of twelve hundred dollars—the value he placed on girls identified as "Susan" and "Margaret." He never got his money. The case was eventually dismissed. What became of the girls? Coffin said they eventually reached freedom in Canada.

Today the Coffin home survives as a historic site. It stands as a reminder of the good that can result when people work together to right injustice. It's a reminder, too, of how much people will risk to be free.

ILLUSTRATOR'S NOTE

Leonard Jenkins's inspiration for the art in this book came from his feelings about the Underground Railroad and slavery. The dark, turbulent sky in this book mirrors the brutality of the slave catchers, and the brighter colors shine through in Hallie's victory over them. Jenkins wanted to depict the past as the colorful and powerful history that it is.

PLACES TO VISIT

Levi Coffin State Historic Site, Fountain City, IN, (765) 847-2432
National Underground Railroad Freedom Center, Cincinnati, OH

RECOMMENDED READING

Bial, Raymond. *The Underground Railroad.* Boston: Houghton Mifflin Company, 1995.
Coffin, Levi. *Reminiscences.* 1876. Reprint, edited by Ben Richmond. Richmond, IN: Friends United Press, 1991.
Haskins, Jim. *Get on Board: The Story of the Underground Railroad.* New York: Scholastic Inc., 1993.
Levine, Ellen. . . . *If You Traveled on the Underground Railroad.* New York: Scholastic Inc., 1988.

WEBSITES

http://www.nationalgeographic.com/railroad
http://www.undergroundrailroad.org
http://www.cr.nps.gov/nr/travel/underground
http://www.indianahistory.org/heritage/levic.html
http://www.in.gov/ism/HistoricSites/LeviCoffin/historic.asp

Text copyright © 2004 by Barbara Olenyik Morrow
Illustrations copyright © 2004 by Leonard Jenkins
All Rights Reserved
Printed in the United States of America
The text typeface is Caslon Antique.
The artwork was created using acrylic, pastel, spray paint, and sometimes colored pencil.
www.holidayhouse.com
First Edition
1 3 5 7 9 10 8 6 4 2
Library of Congress Cataloging-in-Publication Data
Morrow, Barbara Olenyik
A good night for freedom / by Barbara Olenyik Morrow ; illustrated by Leonard Jenkins.—1st ed.
p.   cm.
Summary: Hallie discovers two runaway slaves hiding in Levi Coffin's home and must decide whether to turn them in or help them escape to freedom. Includes historical notes on the Underground Railroad and abolitionists Levi and Catharine Coffin.
ISBN 0-8234-1709-3 (hardcover)
1. Underground railroad—Juvenile fiction. [1. Underground railroad—Fiction. 2. Fugitive slaves—Fiction. 3. Slavery—Fiction. 4. Coffin, Levi, 1798–1877—Fiction.] I. Jenkins, Leonard, ill. II. Title.
PZ7.M84538Go 2004
[E]—dc21   2002192207

I was delivering butter to Aunt Katy—everybody called her that — early that morning in 1839. While she fetched me a coin in another room, I decided to be helpful.

"Takin' the butter to the cellar kitchen," I called, heading down the stairs. I set the crock on the table.

Something stirred. I looked around in the flickering light, then ducked into the spring room. I took two steps, maybe three.

My heart slammed against my chest.

Standing in the darkness were two girls. Our faces were so close little clouds of their breath mixed with mine. They didn't move. Neither did I.

Runaways!

I hadn't known Aunt Katy and Mr. Levi Coffin long—only since last summer when Pa and Mama moved us from Kentucky to Newport, Indiana. But I'd been in Newport long enough to hear the talk that the Coffins helped runaway slaves.

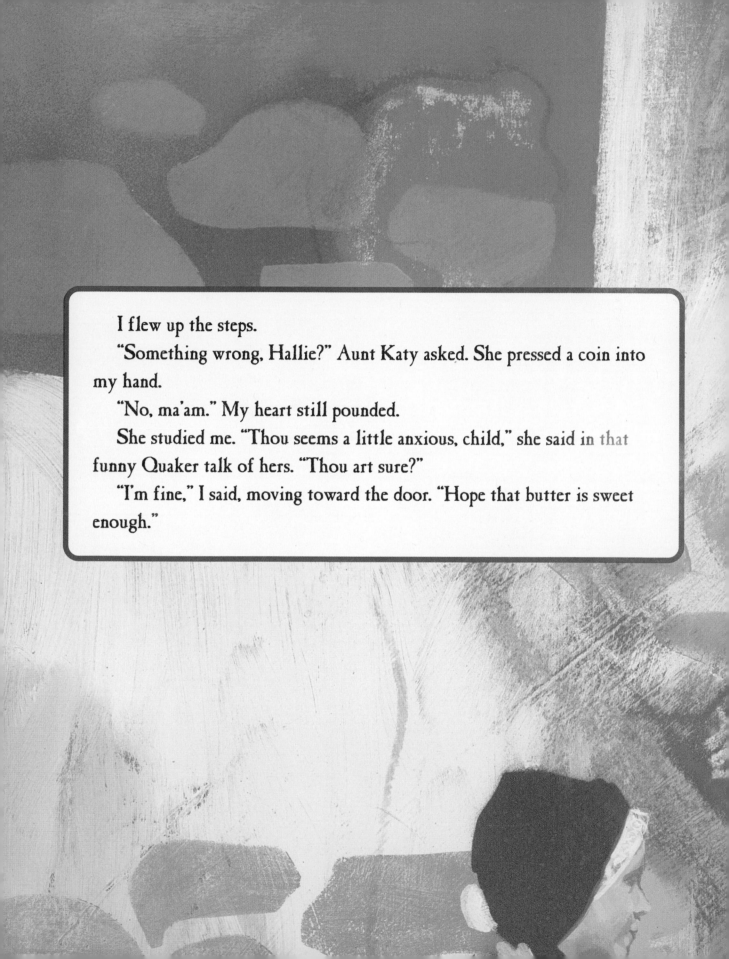

I flew up the steps.

"Something wrong, Hallie?" Aunt Katy asked. She pressed a coin into my hand.

"No, ma'am." My heart still pounded.

She studied me. "Thou seems a little anxious, child," she said in that funny Quaker talk of hers. "Thou art sure?"

"I'm fine," I said, moving toward the door. "Hope that butter is sweet enough."

I raced home, past the gristmill at the edge of town, past fields of stubble, past dark woods with patches of snow. Had those girls hidden in the woods? Had they run through those fields? One looked only about my age, and the other couldn't have been much older. I'd seen slaves before. Plenty, back in Kentucky. But I'd never seen runaways!

From behind, I heard the clop of hooves, then loud voices. Four men, in a hurry, rode up beside me.

"Seen any stray horses?" one called. His whiskery face was covered with dry spittle.

"Seen any stray anything?" another asked. The men snickered.

My eyes lighted on a whip hanging from a saddle. I looked up. The rider, a thick-necked man, smiled. A sugary smile.

"Don't aim to cause you no trouble, missy," he drawled. "Just somethin' for your pa."

He tossed a paper to my feet. His big-knuckled hand fingered the whip. "Want you should take that home." He tipped his hat. "We's obliged."

I didn't wait to see them ride off. As soon as I was in shouting distance of the barn, I hollered, and Pa hurried out. "Four strangers," I panted, waving the paper. Together we read.

$600 Reward!

Ran away from
Tennessee
two Negro girls,
Susan and Margaret,
on the night of
the 2nd of January

I glanced up. "Would you help runaways? I mean, if you knew where those girls were, would you tell?"

Pa peered at me, like he was trying to know my mind.

He began slowly, "I don't like slavery. But there's a law against helpin' runaways. A judge could fine me $500. Or we could find our barn in flames. Those slave catchers have mean ways of warnin' folks not to interfere."

Pa looked back at our house, then at me. "I don't have to like slavery. I don't have to like that law. But I'm not invitin' trouble. Runaways can take care of themselves. We're not meddlin'."

I couldn't shake Pa's words, even later when Mama asked me to deliver food to a sickly neighbor. Afterward, I took a roundabout way home.

When I marched into Levi Coffin's dry goods store, something itched inside me.

Mr. Coffin smiled from behind the counter. "Afternoon, Hallie. How may I help thee?"

I cleared my throat. "Four men came round our farm this mornin'. Slave catchers. Lookin' for runaways."

Mr. Coffin glanced up from his ledger.

"Pa told me there's a law against helpin' runaways. Says folks can get into trouble for helpin'."

What was I doing? Meddlin', Pa would say.

Mr. Coffin laid down his pen. "And what does thou think about that law, Hallie?"

"I . . . I don't know. Pa says the law's the law."

The McArdle family, as loud as they were large, walked in just then. Mr. Coffin stepped quickly around the counter and took me aside. His voice was low, but firm. "It is right to listen to thy father. He's a good man. But thou has a conscience, child. As a Quaker, I—" He stopped, his eyes softening. "Say hello to thy pa, Hallie. Perhaps the three of us can talk another time."

I knew I should go straight home. But my curiosity kept bobbing up like a cork in a rain barrel. From the dry goods store to the Coffins' house wasn't far, just down the street.

Aunt Katy met me at the door.

"I saw the runaways!" I blurted out. "Susan and Margaret."

For the longest time, the only sounds were the porch boards creaking under my fidgety feet. Finally, Aunt Katy pushed open the door. "Come, Hallie. I'd like thee to meet our guests."

Down we went to the cellar kitchen, the smell of chamomile tea sharp in my nose. The girls were at a table. Their faces clouded when they saw me.

"It's all right, girls," Aunt Katy called to them, while nudging me forward. "Take a seat and visit, Hallie. I'll fetch my knitting and be right back."

"But . . ." I shot a sidelong glance toward the spring room.

"No need for hiding right now," Aunt Katy said, reading my mind. "Only when there's trouble." She disappeared up the steps.

I fiddled in my pocket with the coin Aunt Katy had given me that morning, and suddenly it flipped out and clinked across the floor. Susan — or was it Margaret? — slapped it down with her foot. She snatched it up.

"That's mine."

My voice startled even me.

"I earned that coin," I said. "I churn butter, and Mama lets me sell extra. I plan to buy ribbon. Red ribbon."

A look passed between them, then they turned my way, seeming to take measure. Could I be trusted? Why was I there? Their eyes bored into me, past my jaw set tight.

A chair scraped. The girl with my coin stood.

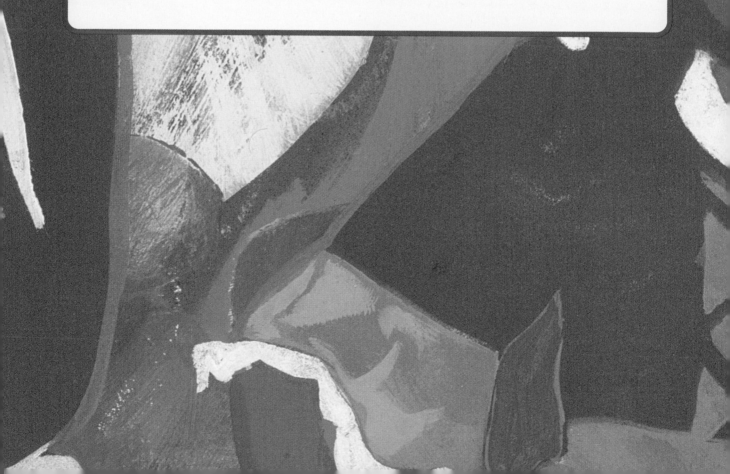

"When I get to freedom, aim to get me a payin' job," she said. "Gonna earn buckets of coins."

"What you fixin' on buyin'?"

"Mama." She sucked in her breath. "Master sold her. Sister and I got to get her back."

The words stung me like that slave catcher's whip might have.

"How you goin' to do that? Get your mama, I mean?"

"Don't know. Got to get to freedom first." She held out the coin.

I dropped my head. "You keep it."

"Don't want it. It's yours."

She giant-stepped toward me, arm still out, hand open.

"Sorry," I said, reaching slowly for the coin. "Sorry I can't help your mama."

Suddenly footsteps rang out above us, and Mr. Coffin shouted for Aunt Katy. He hurried down the stairs and hustled the girls out of sight.

"Straight home, child," he said to me. "Thy pa will be worried."

The door was barely bolted behind me when I saw the four men, riding fast. A circle of folks gathered across the street. I edged in among them.

Horses snorted, reins jerked. The men jumped from their saddles and started pounding hard on the Coffins' door.

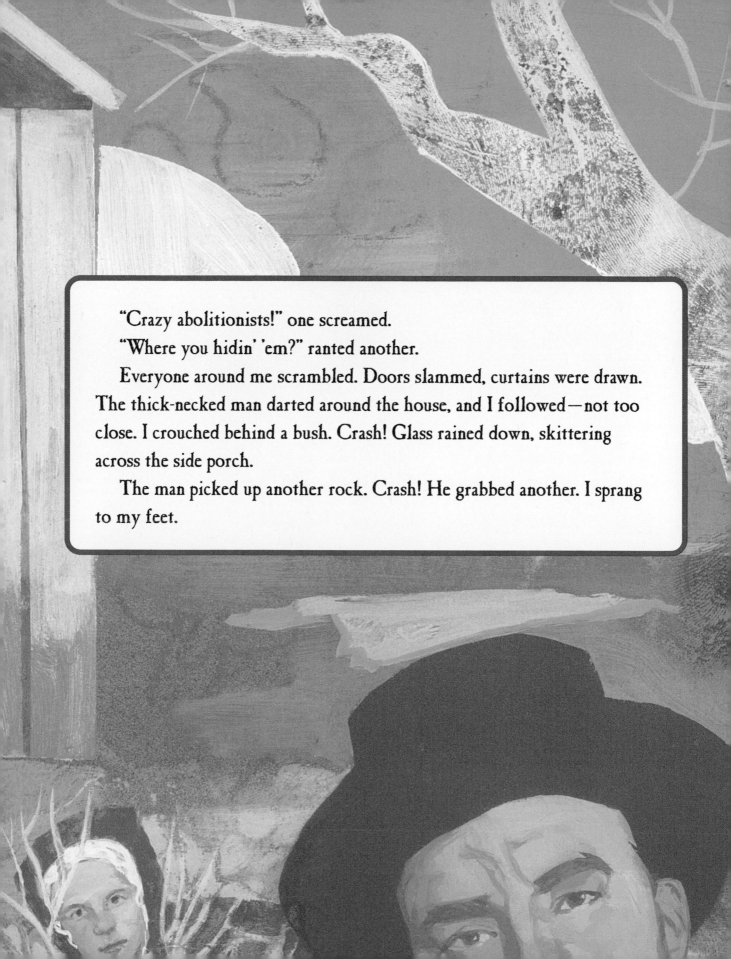

"Crazy abolitionists!" one screamed.

"Where you hidin' 'em?" ranted another.

Everyone around me scrambled. Doors slammed, curtains were drawn. The thick-necked man darted around the house, and I followed—not too close. I crouched behind a bush. Crash! Glass rained down, skittering across the side porch.

The man picked up another rock. Crash! He grabbed another. I sprang to my feet.

"I saw them." The words spat from my mouth.

"Hallie!" Mr. Coffin threw open the door, pulling it tight behind him. "Child!" he warned.

"I saw two girls headin' up the Winchester Road. This mornin'. They cut across the pasture, then into the woods."

The man came closer. "You saw two of 'em? Headin' north?"

"Yes, sir."

"Him there, did he tell you to say that?"

I gulped. "No, sir. He didn't."

The man gave a cold, sassy laugh, then glared at Mr. Coffin. "Mighty fine rock," he said, hurling it toward the porch. Glass shattered, splinters flew. "Saddle up," he ordered the others.

I squeezed my eyes shut.

"Up the Winchester Road, right?" He jerked my shoulder.

I raised my arm and pointed.

And then he was gone. Really gone.

My knees went soft, and I slumped to the ground. A gentle hand touched my head.

"I meddled," I said, looking up into Mr. Coffin's face.

A long silence passed. Cupping my chin in his hand, Mr. Coffin smiled, then walked slowly toward the house. "Thank thee, child," he called back softly.

I thought about what he had said in his store, about conscience.

I thought about Pa.

"Why'd you get mixed up in that, Hallie?" I figured he'd ask, sounding none too pleased. And not pleasing Pa, well . . . I didn't feel good about that.

But Pa himself called me strong-minded. And if that means thinking for myself—if it's doing what I believe is right when others, even Pa, might not agree—then that's what I am.

And brave is what I'd try to be.

Brave, like Susan and Margaret, is what I *aimed* to be.

I lifted my arms and stretched high, higher. Then I leaned back my head to drink in the late afternoon sky.

Clear night ahead, I reckoned. Starry night, good night. For running, for hoping, for being—almost—free.